being God's man...
by finding contentment

the every man series

Real Men. Real Life. Powerful Truth.

Stephen Arterburn

Kenny Luck & Todd Wendorff

WATERBROOK
PRESS

BEING GOD'S MAN...BY FINDING CONTENTMENT
PUBLISHED BY WATERBROOK PRESS
2375 Telstar Drive, Suite 160
Colorado Springs, Colorado 80920
A division of Random House, Inc.

ISBN 1-57856-916-8

Published in association with the literary agency of Alive Communications, Inc., 7680 Goddard Street, Suite 200, Colorado Springs, CO 80920.

Printed in the United States of America
2004—First Edition

10 9 8 7 6 5 4 3 2 1

contents

welcome to the every man
Bible study series

As Christian men, we crave true-to-life, honest, and revealing Bible study curricula that will equip us for the battles that rage in our lives. We are looking for resources that will get us into our Bibles in the context of mutually accountable relationships with other men. But like superheroes who wear masks and work hard to conceal their true identities, most of us find ourselves isolated and working alone on the major issues we face. Many of us present a carefully designed public self while hiding our private self from view. This is not God's plan for us.

Let's face it. We all have trouble being honest with ourselves, particularly in front of other men.

As developers of a men's ministry, we believe that many of the problems among Christian men today are direct consequences of an inability to practice biblical openness—being honest about our struggles, questions, and temptations—and to connect with one another. Our external lives may be in order, but storms of unprocessed conflict, loss, and fear are eroding our resolve to maintain integrity. Sadly, hurting Christian men are flocking to unhealthy avenues of relief instead of turning to God's Word and to one another.

We believe the solution to this problem lies in creating opportunities for meaningful relationships among men. That's why we designed this Bible study series to be thoroughly interactive. When a man practices biblical openness with other men, he moves from secrecy to candor, from isolation to connection, and from pretense to authenticity.

Kenny and Todd developed the study sessions at Saddleback Church in Lake Forest, California, and at King's Harbor Church in Redondo Beach, California, where they teach men's Bible studies. At these studies men hear an outline of the Bible passage, read the verses together, and then answer a group discussion question at their small-group tables. The teaching pastor then facilitates further discussion within the larger group.

This approach is a huge success for many reasons, but the key is that, deep down, men really do want close friendships with other guys. We don't enjoy living on the barren islands of our own secret struggles. However, many men choose to process life, relationships, and pressures individually because they fear the vulnerability required in small-group gatherings. *Suppose someone sees behind my carefully constructed image? Suppose I encounter rejection after revealing one of my worst sins?* Men willingly take risks in business and the stock market, sports and recreation, but we do not easily risk our inner lives.

Many church ministries are now helping men win this battle, providing them with opportunities to experience Christian male companionship centered in God's Word. This study series aims to supplement and expand that good work around the country. If these lessons successfully reach you, then they will also reach every relationship and domain that you influence. That is our heartfelt prayer for every man in your group.

how to use this study guide

As you prepare for each session, first review the **Key Verse** and **Goals for Growth,** which reveal the focus of the study at hand. Discuss as a group whether or not you will commit to memorizing the Key Verse for each session. The **Head Start** section then explains why these goals are necessary and worthwhile. Each member of your small group should complete the **Connect with the Word** section *before* the small-group sessions. Consider this section to be your personal Bible study for the week. This will ensure that everyone has spent some time interacting with the biblical texts for that session and is prepared to share responses and personal applications. (You may want to mark or highlight any questions that were difficult or particularly meaningful so you can focus on those during the group discussion.)

When you gather in your small group, you'll begin by reading aloud the **Head Start** section to remind everyone of the focus for the current session. The leader will then invite the group to share any questions, concerns, insights, or comments arising from their personal Bible study during the past week. If your group is large, consider breaking into subgroups of three or four people (no more than six) at this time.

Next, get into **Connect with the Group,** starting with the **Group Opener.** These openers are designed to get at the heart of each week's lesson. They focus on how the men in your group relate to the passage and topic you are about to discuss. The group leader will read aloud the opener for that week's session and then facilitate interaction on the **Discussion Questions** that follow. (Remember: Not everyone has to offer an answer for every question.)

Leave time after your discussion to complete the **Standing Strong** exercises, which challenge each man to consider, *What's my next move?* As you openly express your thoughts to the group, you'll be able to hold one another accountable to reach for your goals.

Finally, close in **prayer,** either in your subgroups or in the larger group. You may want to use this time to reflect on and respond to what God has done in your group during the session. Also invite group members to share their personal joys and concerns, and use this as "grist" for your prayer time together.

By way of review, each lesson is divided into the following sections:

To be read or completed *before* the small-group session:
- **Key Verse**
- **Goals for Growth**
- **Head Start**
- **Connect with the Word** (home Bible study: 30-40 minutes)

To be completed *during* the small-group session:
- Read aloud the **Head Start** section (5 minutes)
- Discuss personal reaction to **Connect with the Word** (10 minutes)
- **Connect with the Group** (includes the **Group Opener** and discussion of the heart of the lesson: 30-40 minutes)
- **Standing Strong** (includes having one person pray for the group; challenges each man to take action: 20 minutes)

wrestling with God

As men, we find it tough to be content with what we have. We compare ourselves with others—whether it's our job, our wife, our child's performance, our looks, or even our talent—and often find ourselves coming up short. The by-product of comparison is discontentment.

Some of us blame God for not giving us what we presume to be "what's best for me." We determine to get it, and life becomes a struggle of the discontented heart. And age doesn't seem to matter. I've seen men in their seventies and eighties still searching for more to fill their aching hearts.

The truth is, contentment comes from a heart change, a change of mind-set, and a willing choice. Yes, only a transformation of mind, emotions, and will can bring about lasting contentment in a man's heart. It also takes a personal encounter with the One who can make a man content. When God gets hold of a man, he becomes a new creature. He finds refuge in the Lord and recognizes that what God has given him is for his benefit and enjoyment. He learns to trust that the Lord knows exactly what he needs and cares about every desire. No one else can know him like that. God's man realizes that to experience true contentment, he must meet the Lord Himself.

What I've just described is a struggle for a new identity, as the Bible's story of Jacob shows us. Jacob saw himself as a deceiver his entire life—until he met with the Lord and laid his past to rest. One blow from the Lord ended Jacob's struggle. In that moment of brokenness, Jacob said to himself, "I saw God face to face, and yet my life was spared" (Genesis 32:30). Jacob became a new person, a father to the nations, a man on a mission for the Lord. His struggle was over; he knew why he was here and what he had to do. Even in the midst of immense grief over a lost son (Joseph), he knew God's purposes in his life would not be thwarted. (See Genesis 37:34-35.) God now had mastery over Jacob's heart and his core identity.

In effect, Jacob became a man fully released from striving after unfulfilled expectations and lost dreams. His life took on purpose and meaning that transcended striving. He knew his calling, and it was a heavenly one. The scattered pieces of Jacob's life finally came together, and God even gave him a new name. He died fully content in the Lord.

Have the pieces of your life come together yet? Or are you still controlled by scattered events, shattered dreams, and only occasional moments of contentment? Finding contentment with who you are and why you're here may not happen for you as it did for Jacob. It may take longer than one momentous encounter with God. It may thrust you into a season of wrestling and striving. But every man must walk the same path: discontentment, struggle, an encounter with God, a new identity, contentment.

In his 1648 work *The Rare Jewel of Christian Contentment,* Jeremiah Burroughs wrote that "contentment in every condition is a great art, a spiritual mystery. It is to be learned and to be learned as a mystery." By this he meant that the mystery of contentment lies in God's ability to change us. We cannot manufacture contentment on our own. It takes a willing soul to desire this inward change of heart and disposition. "Christian contentment," Burroughs observed, "is that sweet, inward, quiet, gracious frame of spirit, which freely submits to and delights in God's wise and fatherly disposal in every condition." Content is the man who is at peace with, fully submitted to, and happy in God.

It is rare to find a man completely satisfied with what God has given him. Yet pity the man who never finds his contentment in the Lord. He travels a course of self-destruction. Life's circumstances make him a target for worry and disappointment. He is robbed of a life focused on the Lord's priorities.

Our goal in this study is to stimulate personal reflection and honest dialogue with God and other men about the topic of contentment. As you work through each session, look in the mirror at your own life and ask yourself some hard questions. Whether you are doing this study individually or in a group, realize that being completely honest with yourself, with God, and with others will produce the greatest growth.

Our prayer is that as you wrestle with God in the area of contentment, you will stop comparing yourself with others and searching for contentment in things that will never satisfy. When you encounter God on a personal level and allow Him to transform your heart, mind, and emotions, you will discover the lasting peace and contentment that He alone can give. May you find true contentment as you seek to be completely satisfied with what God has given you and with who He has created you to be.

accept it!

Wanting Nothing More, Nothing Less

Key Verses

I know what it is to be in need, and I know what it is to have plenty. I have learned the secret of being content in any and every situation, whether well fed or hungry, whether living in plenty or in want. I can do everything through him who gives me strength. (Philippians 4:12-13)

Goals for Growth

- Identify areas of discontentment in my life.
- Learn to hand over control of my life to God in the moment.
- Desire nothing more or nothing less than what God has given me.

Head Start

Contentment doesn't mean we don't have any troubles. (That's obvious! Just review your life over the past week.) Contentment simply means that we rock with the rolls and slide with the downpours. Paul learned that a man will be up and a man will be down. Whether we are up or down, we can be content in whatever circumstances God has allowed us to face.

We often think we are where we are by fate or ill will or for some other unknown reason and that God had nothing to do with it. *Certainly, God wouldn't want me in this mess!* we think. *I must get myself out of this—now!* That's when we get into trouble. We become discontented and we struggle to break free. We take our eyes off God and often end up drifting out into deeper water—and an even bigger mess.

Contentment also doesn't mean that we ride out the storms of life alone. Each of us needs the support and encouragement of other men in challenging times. A ship can't drift through a storm unattended. It takes a crew to get its bow pointed into the storm, to hold it steady as it plows through rough waves. Paul learned to lean on others so he could make it through seemingly impossible situations.

Are waves crashing in on you from all directions? Do you feel all alone, adrift in the midst of your troubles? You're not the only man who feels this way. I (Todd) have found that whenever I get men together and ask them to talk about their struggles, they quickly realize they're not alone. Their struggles mirror those of the guy sitting next to them. Their problems, as difficult as they may seem, are hardly unique.

What painful circumstance is testing your contentment in the

Lord these days? What is draining contentment from your veins? How you handle these challenges will reveal where you place your trust—in God, in yourself, in others, or in your circumstances.

Ships need a captain. So do our lives. We often declare mutiny against God at the first sign of discontentment, but every good seaman knows that storms are part of the open seas. Ride them out and learn to trust the One in charge. Jeremiah Burroughs said, "The righteous man can never be made so poor, to have his house so rifled and spoiled, but there will remain much treasure within."

Did you catch that? The treasure remains within. Even when all is lost, the treasure remains.

As David, the psalmist, said, "It was good for me to be afflicted" (Psalm 119:71). In his afflictions he learned this: Only what remains after the rifling and the spoiling matters. Can you take up the quiet confidence that what God will leave behind in your heart after the storm is the rare jewel of contentment? After all is said and done, it's all that really matters.

Connect with the Word

Read Philippians 4:10-19.

1. What different life circumstances did Paul identify in this passage? Which comes closest to your own experience? Explain.

2. What made it possible for Paul not to be "in need" (verse 11)?

3. How do you think Christ strengthened him (verse 13)?

4. Read the following scriptures and list one truth from each about being strengthened in Christ.

   2 Corinthians 12:9

   Ephesians 3:16

   Colossians 1:11-12

5. How did the Philippians help Paul through his struggles (verses 14-18)?

6. What did Paul say in verses 17 and 18 about the true value of letting others help us in times of trouble?

7. Check out 2 Corinthians 1:6-11 and 4:7-18 to see how Paul responded in his most difficult times. What do you learn from Paul's example? Which of Paul's attitudes and actions can you apply to your own life?

8. In light of the fact that Paul talked about making it through his own troubles in verses 10-18, why do you think he shifted from "me" to "you" in verse 19?

Connect with the Group

Group Opener

Read the group opener aloud and discuss the questions that follow. (Suggestion: As you begin your group discussion time in each of the following sessions, consider forming smaller groups of three to six men. This will allow more time for discussion and give everyone an opportunity to share their thoughts and struggles.)

Leaning on his fence one day, a devout Quaker was watching a new neighbor move in next door. After all kinds of modern appliances, electronic gadgets, plush furniture, and costly wall hangings had been carried into the house, the onlooker called, "If you find you're lacking anything, neighbor, let me know and I'll show you how to live without it."

Frightening thought, isn't it? Yet it is amazing what you can live without if you really think about it.

My wife and I (Todd) were driving our rusted-out Toyota Cressida (with 195,000 miles on the odometer) on one of the Chicago toll roads when I noticed a new, top-of-the-line BMW to our left. I looked over and said to Denise, "They must be rich, don't you think? And yet the only difference between them and us is the *cost* of the automobile they drive, the *quality* of the food they eat, and the *size* of house they live in."

Otherwise, the man driving that Beemer and I are probably a lot alike. He likely works five days a week (maybe more), eats three meals a day, and puts his pants on in the morning one leg at a time. He no doubt gets vacation time and probably enjoys walking in the forest preserve with his family in the fall just as much as I do.

The truth is, being content with what you have is all a matter of perspective. Families who live in apartments or small older homes can enjoy life as much as those who live in three-story mansions. Jeremiah Burroughs said, "A little in this world will content a Christian for his passage." A little is all we need to make it through this life to the next. Actually, living with less leads to greater contentment and helps us gain a new perspective on life.

Discussion Questions

a. Do you agree that the differences between the BMW man and the Cressida man are insignificant? Why or why not?

b. When have you been the most content with the least? When have you suffered discontentment in the midst of plenty? What did you learn from these experiences?

c. What advice would you give a younger man who is striving to have as much as his neighbor does?

d. When you are most tempted to be discontent, what is usually the issue: possessions, career, relationships, or something else? Talk about it.

e. Finish the following sentences:

I am most content when. . .

I am least content when. . .

f. To whom or what are you turning for help in your current circumstances? Why?

Standing Strong

In the space provided below, describe a situation you are facing that is making it hard for you to be content. Ask the man next to you to pray for you about this situation. Then pray for him about the situation he is facing.

can money buy contentment?

Looking for Contentment in All the Wrong Places

Key Verse

The love of money is a root of all kinds of evil. Some people, eager for money, have wandered from the faith and pierced themselves with many griefs. (1 Timothy 6:10)

Goals for Growth

- Learn to trust God with my future.
- Be willing to give up short-term desires for long-term gain.
- Refocus my attention on things that matter most.

Head Start

Godly men are content men.

Why is that? Is it because they don't struggle like the rest of us? Or is it because they're too busy studying their Bibles to realize they have real problems like you and I do? If that's the case, then maybe godly men are living in denial. Maybe they're too spiritual—so heavenly minded they're no earthly good. Or maybe they've arrived at a "deeper level of consciousness."

But none of these explanations hits the mark. No, godly men live in the same world we do, and they deal with the same struggles. They just hold a different view about what is ultimately important in life. Developing their relationship with the Lord has become more important to them than worrying about whether they have enough money stored away for the future. It's not that they don't concern themselves with finances, car repairs, college education for the kids, and retirement. They've just learned to focus on another goal in life: their personal godliness.

You might be thinking, *This form of godliness is unattainable for me! I'm not wired that way. If I don't worry about my future, I won't have one.*

But this kind of thinking is faulty. The problem lies not in the fact that we are concerned about the future but that our perception of godliness is off. Godliness doesn't mean we stick our heads in the sand or become oblivious to real problems and concerns. Rather, it means we keep the bigger picture in view: We are citizens of God's kingdom, living out our Lord's values in all we do (even if it's planning for retirement). And by focusing on the right thing—the perspective of God's Word—we're able to move beyond discontentment.

In the Bible passage you are about to study, Paul contrasted right doctrine (God's truth) with the pursuit of money. You might think this is an odd contrast. But you are either pursuing the truth that

God is the Source of your contentment or the deception that says money is the source of happiness.

Paul wasn't saying we have to take a vow of poverty to attain godliness. He was simply saying that a godly man finds new perspective about his future in God's Word. A godly man learns to be content pursuing matters of eternal value. He has fully embraced this truth: "I came into the world with nothing, and I will leave it with nothing...except whatever treasures I've stored up in heaven." After all, "a man's life does not consist in the abundance of his possessions" (Luke 12:15).

What are you pursuing? Material things or something more lasting—godliness? It alone brings contentment. Focus on that.

Connect with the Word

Read 1 Timothy 6:3-21.

1. What kind of man is described in verses 3-5?

2. How does knowing good doctrine (God's truth from the Bible) help a man stay focused on the right things?

3. How can you make sure that good doctrine settles permanently into your mind and heart? Be specific.

4. Does godliness produce contentment or does contentment produce godliness (verse 6)? How are they related?

5. Define *contentment* based on verses 7 and 8.

6. In what ways can riches trap you? When are you most likely to become entangled?

7. How has your pursuit of wealth affected your pursuit of truth? Can you pursue both at the same time? Why or why not?

8. What is God's man told to pursue in verse 11? How can pursuing these qualities keep you from being stained by the world?

9. In what way is the struggle to find contentment related to fighting "the good fight of the faith" (verse 12)?

10. What is the antidote to fixing our hopes on riches (verses 17-19)?

Connect with the Group

Group Opener
Read the group opener aloud and discuss the questions that follow.

I (Todd) grew up on a hill where almost every home sat on more than an acre overlooking the lights of Los Angeles. One of the core beliefs of those who lived on this hill was "money equals happiness." The more you have, the better the quality of your life.

That wasn't the belief of Mike Toll, even though he, too, lived on the hill. Mike was a successful builder and had many of the things this world offers: a nice home, a tennis court in his backyard, an airplane, a racing boat called *Snoopy*, and a great family. He had two offices, one in Los Angeles and one in Phoenix, and he would fly his plane back and forth. He lived a dream life.

But Mike lived for something else; he was a man who walked with God. During the recession of the '70s, Mike was criticized for keeping his employees on his payroll even though he had no work for them. "It's not good business practice," some would say. Yet Mike knew these people had families and wouldn't be able to find other jobs. He cared about them and showed it in his actions.

Mike didn't seem to worry much about the future. It was in God's hands. He lived by his biblical convictions, and it showed. He always had a smile on his face and a warm greeting for others. No matter the circumstances, he always kept a godly perspective and cared for others before himself.

A few years after the economy turned around, Mike died in a plane crash as he was flying to his office in Arizona. He called in to the tower minutes before his plane went down in the desert. He had a choice: bring the plane down on a crowded freeway or attempt to land in an open field. He chose the field.

After his funeral, I was talking with his wife, Bonny. She told me that after Mike died, she sat at his desk and looked at the verses Mike had collected and underlined in his Bible. She said he would sit there day after day and read those verses. It was his regular routine. We lost a good man that day.

Whether you live on a hill or in the valley or on the flatlands, you probably wrestle with your future. Will my family and I be able to continue living at our current standard? Will we be able to buy everything we want or need? Will we be able to do all the things we're planning to do?

We all struggle with where we will find contentment. Jeremiah Burroughs wrote, "A Christian comes to contentment, not so much by way of addition, as by way of subtraction." Have you determined to live by that heavenly arithmetic?

Discussion Questions

a. Do you know of anyone like Mike? What qualities do you most admire in that person?

b. What do you think made that person godly? How do you think he's been able to overcome a narrow perception of reality in order to live as a kingdom person?

c. Why is it important to overcome the deceptive, narrow view that "godliness is a means to financial gain" (1 Timothy 6:5)?

d. When are you most tempted to fret about money? What can a man do to prevent the discontentment that comes from a life focused on material gain? (See 1 Timothy 6:17-19.)

e. When have you seen the workings of "heavenly arithmetic" in your life?

Standing Strong

In the space provided below, first list the amount of money and personal assets you believe would be sufficient for your personal needs now, for the next twenty years, and for your retirement. Then list the stresses that your responses for each category might be causing you. Finally, in light of today's Scripture passage, describe your antidote for each of the stresses you identified.

What I need now:

Related stresses:

Antidote:

What I'll need for the next twenty years:

Related stresses:

Antidote:

What I'll need for retirement:

Related stresses:

Antidote:

worry won't get you anywhere

Eliminating the Anxious Heart

Key Verse

I tell you, do not worry about your life, what you will eat or drink; or about your body, what you will wear. Is not life more important than food, and the body more important than clothes? (Matthew 6:25)

Goals for Growth

- Begin to eliminate thoughts that lead to worry.
- Realize that God will provide all my needs.
- Shift my focus off myself and onto God's kingdom.

Head Start

Worry is a telltale sign of a discontented heart. We worry when we feel that God has somehow dropped the ball and become preoccupied with more pressing issues, leaving us to handle life alone.

When we feel this way, we need to remind ourselves of the full abilities of our God. He is omnipresent, omnipotent, and omniscient. That means He's always present in all places at all times, He's all-powerful and in complete control, and He knows everything. He can handle the cosmos; He can also handle our daily agendas. No doubt that's why Jesus said the only antidote for a worried heart is a new focus. (See Matthew 6:33.) We can either focus on our troubles or we can focus on God, who is fully capable of caring for us.

Someone once said that worry is taking on a responsibility that God never intended us to have. Men love to take charge, but our greatest strength can also be our greatest weakness. What often accompanies our taking charge is worry. We worry about the details. We worry about whether we have the resources necessary to get the job done. We worry when things don't go according to plan.

I (Todd) was on the phone with a friend the other day, and he said, "Somebody just shoot me. I have a to-do list a mile long, and I'm getting nowhere fast. It's hopeless."

Worry hits the best of us, but it shouldn't. We succumb to worry only when we think we have to take charge. That's why I love how Jesus convinces us to give Him back the reins. He simply tells us to look at the birds: "They do not sow or reap or store away in barns, and yet your heavenly Father feeds them. Are you not much more valuable than they?" (Matthew 6:26). That puts things in perspective!

Can you imagine the task of feeding and housing all the birds of the sky? I grew up hunting birds with my dad and brother. We've hunted in places where the birds were so thick you couldn't see the sky above them. I can't imagine caring for every single bird that occupies the entire earth and sky.

What about trying to count all the hairs on your head or all the grains of sand on the beach? How would you even begin to do that? But God has every bird, every hair, and every grain of sand accounted for. So sit back and relax!

Why do we get so worked up over what's going to happen next in our lives? God knows each of us by name. And He scheduled each of our days before we even began to breathe. Surely He can handle the details of our lives!

What's keeping you from turning your worries over to Him?

Connect with the Word

Read Matthew 6:25–34.

1. How would you define *worry?* In what areas of your life is it most prevalent?

2. What, specifically, are we not to worry about (verse 25)?

3. Why is it difficult to fully trust God with all our needs, even the most basic ones?

4. Why do you think Jesus went into such detail about God's care for the birds of the air? How does this encourage you?

5. What does it mean, in practical terms, to "seek first [God's] kingdom and his righteousness" (verse 33)?

6. Do you know anyone who has lived this out? What can you do to emulate this person's approach to life?

Connect with the Group

Group Opener
Read the group opener aloud and discuss the questions that follow.

The freedom now desired by many is not freedom to do an dare but freedom from care and worry.

—James Truslow Adams

Do you agree or disagree with this statement? Why?

How does it apply to you personally?

How would you rewrite this statement to make it more relevant or applicable to your own life situation? (For example: "The freedom I now desire is not the ability to complete my to-do list, but the ability to rest in knowing that God will get me through this day.")

Discussion Questions

a. Of the areas mentioned in Matthew 6:25, which do you worry about most? What aspects of your upbringing or personality might contribute to this tendency? Explain.

b. Think about growing up in your family. To what extent was your father a worrier? In what ways, if any, has this affected you as an adult?

c. Matthew 6:26 implies that we are the most valuable of all created things. How does this help you deal with worry?

d. Recall a time when you were most worried or doubtful about God's care for you. What attitudes or circumstances contributed to your worry or doubt?

e. What spiritual truths did you learn from the experiences you described in questions b and d?

f. What steps will you take to seek God's kingdom first?

Standing Strong

Say good-bye to worry. Practice the discipline of letting go of worry when it surfaces in your heart and mind. Don't let it get the best of you.

In the space provided, write down all the things you could ever worry about. Then based on the passage you have just studied, write down what God says about you and His concern for you.

Things I Worry About	*What God Says About Me*

heaven bound, hassle free

Being Content—Because of Heaven

Key Verse

One thing I ask of the LORD, this is what I seek: that I may dwell in the house of the LORD all the days of my life, to gaze upon the beauty of the LORD and to seek him in his temple. (Psalm 27:4)

Goals for Growth

- Set my gaze in this life heavenward.
- Find hope in my eternal destination in the here and now.
- See my hardships as temporary.

Head Start

Heaven may seem a far-off place, a distant future, and a far cry from the pressures of the office or a Saturday filled with household chores.

Yet heaven is our destination, and a heavenward gaze brings contentment and confidence to the godly man.

How true this was of the great Christian apologist and literature professor C. S. Lewis! He once said that when he arrives in heaven, the first thing he will say is, "Of course!" Of course heaven is what it is. And we'll recognize it when we see it if we live life here on earth with heaven in focus. But this requires that we learn contentment while we're here.

"Most people," said Lewis in *Mere Christianity,* "if they had really learned to look into their own hearts, would know that they do want, and want acutely, something that cannot be had in this world." Does that ring true for you? Do you sense a holy longing that won't be satisfied here? Then let it draw your gaze upward. Recognize that you're not home yet but are headed to the place where all will be well. Can you live moment by moment in that truth?

C. S. Lewis wrote a lot about heaven in his lifetime. It was, as he said, what he was made for. Heaven is a better place, our true home to come, and that prospect comforts the heart and soul in the meantime. Writing of finally arriving there, Lewis said through Jewel the Unicorn in *The Last Battle,* "I have come home at last! This is my real country! I belong here. This is the land I have been looking for all my life, though I never knew it till now. The reason why we loved the old Narnia is that it sometimes looked a little like this. Bree-hee-hee! Come further up, come further in."

More than three hundred years ago, another man set his gaze on heaven. Brother Lawrence, a one-of-a-kind monk, moved into a monastery and served as the dishwasher. It was there he learned the secret to contentment: keeping the presence of the Lord continually before him, even in the midst of clanging pots and pans. In his book *The Practice of the Presence of God,* Brother Lawrence revealed that his amazing, deep-souled contentment blossomed from a constant focus heavenward. As the psalmist put it, "I have set the LORD always before me. Because he is at my right hand, I will not be shaken" (Psalm 16:8). Maybe there's something to the psalms after all—something we missed in Sunday school. Are they not an awesome primer for men learning to be content?

Connect with the Word

Read Psalm 84:10-12.

1. How did the psalmist express his delight in God's presence?

2. Have you ever spent time just "being" in the presence of God? Describe that experience. What benefits might you experience if you made this a meaningful part of your prayer time?

3. What did the psalmist mean when he said that God is "a sun and shield" (verse 11)? In what ways is God a sun and a shield in your own life?

Read Psalm 27:4-6.

4. In this passage the psalmist is speaking about heaven. What words did he use to describe heaven? Why do you think he described it in earthly terms?

5. How can we be "hidden" in heaven while we're on earth? When, if ever, have you felt protected like that?

6. How can the prospect of heaven create contentment in our hearts here and now?

7. Read Paul's words in 2 Corinthians 5:1-10. What comfort do you find in Paul's references to heaven in this passage?

Connect with the Group

Group Opener
Read the group opener aloud and discuss the questions that follow.

C. S. Lewis believed that every desire is at its root a desire for heaven.... We are all pilgrims in search of the Celestial City: some lost and looking for joy in all the wrong places, some saved with eyes fixed on the heavenly prize, some sidetracked on dead-end streets and byways—but all longing for heaven, whether we know it or not. Nearly all of Lewis's works have the aim of arousing this desire for heaven or showing us how to live in proper anticipation of our true home.

—WAYNE MARTINDALE

Discussion Questions

a. Think of your own desires. Do you think all your desires will be satisfied in heaven? Explain.

b. When have you most strongly felt a longing for heaven? What was happening in your life at the time that prompted this longing?

c. In what ordinary life experiences does this longing come through? (For example, mowing the lawn, helping your wife with household chores, watching your kids play sports, working a forty-hour week, and so on.) Explain.

d. Why do you think we tend to separate our experience on earth from our anticipation of heaven? What's the danger in doing that?

e. Psalms 27 and 84 indicate that a foretaste of heaven can help us live a more content life here and now. Is this the case with you? Explain.

f. What tends to hold you back from fully embracing a heavenly perspective? What can other guys do to help you "practice the presence of God" each day?

g. Reflect on Revelation 21:9-27. Are you more anxious or less anxious after reflecting on heaven? Explain.

Standing Strong

Imagine heaven in comparison to the life you are currently living. What do you think are the major differences?

My Life Now	*My Life in Heaven*

Think a little more about what you expect heaven to be like. What aspects of this vision could you incorporate into your daily experience now?

worst-case scenario

Realizing You're Not in Charge

Key Verse

I know that you can do all things; no plan of yours can be thwarted. (Job 42:2)

Goals for Growth

- Learn to see God as unchangeable and sovereign in all my circumstances.
- Be willing to trade the "perfect" life for contentment in the Lord.
- Stop fighting against God's plan for my life.

Head Start

It was one of the scariest experiences of my (Todd's) childhood. I was camping with my family at Lake Mojave and was out on the lake in a small motorized fishing boat, towing my brother, Dave, behind me on a raft. Without warning dark clouds rolled in and the wind picked up, churning up the waves. The situation went from good to bad to worse in seconds. Dave let go of the tow rope and drifted away from me into the whitecaps. Then the boat motor stalled, and I couldn't get it started again. My mom stood on shore screaming, and my dad frantically jumped into our ski boat. I totally panicked. For a moment I didn't know whether to keep trying to start the motor or jump in to save my frightened brother.

That's the way life is for many men. It often seems to go from good to bad to worse in just seconds. Without warning the storm clouds roll in, the wind howls, and the waves whip up. But how does expecting the worst to happen affect our level of contentment? Do we continue to trust God no matter what? Or do we seek to grab control of the situation?

Consider Job's situation for a minute. Could any man have it as bad as he did? He was successful, married, and had plenty of kids. But it didn't stay that way. Every man's worst-case scenario came to pass: Job lost it all. (See Job 1–2.)

Do you know anyone like Job who has lost everything—his children, his job, his home, his savings, even his health—and yet has been able to maintain his confidence in the Lord? Job was able to endure the worst of times because he had the right view of himself and God.

Job reminds me of the priest in the movie *Rudy.* Rudy Ruettiger, a short, stocky football player, wanted to attend Notre Dame so he could play for the Fighting Irish. One problem: Everything was stacked against him. Desperate, he went to church to pray. There he bumped into Father Cavanaugh and asked him for advice. The priest had this to offer: "Son, in thirty-five years of religious studies, I've come up with only two incontrovertible facts: There is a God, and I am not Him." In a sense Father Cavanaugh was saying that you can only do so much. The rest is in God's hands.

Contentment lies in understanding that you are not in charge of the universe—you were never expected to be. Job got it. And in the end he died full of years and filled with peace. Rudy got it too. He never gave up.

The secret of life lies not in holding on to what we have. It's all about holding on to the One who owns it all.

Connect with the Word

Read Job 1:6-22; 42:1-6,10-16.

1. What did Job believe about God as a result of all he went through in life?

2. How do you think his new understanding of God made Job a more content man?

3. In Job 42, a conversation takes place between God and Job at the end of Job's ordeal. Job realizes that his perspective of his situation was off. In what way was it off?

4. Before his ordeal, Job knew God from afar. After his ordeal, he knew God intimately. What was Job's response (42:1-6)?

5. Why do you think God restored most of the things Job had lost—and much more? What does this reveal about God's nature?

6. How does Job's story help you trust God more in your daily life?

Connect with the Group

Group Opener
Read the group opener aloud and discuss the questions that follow.

When I (Todd) first met Barry, he was in an on-again, off-again relationship with Karen, a cute female student from San Diego State University. She had been discipled by my wife and was growing in her relationship with the Lord. Barry had a sacrificial love for Karen and would do anything for her. Not surprisingly they married.

Following a successful run with a real-estate developer, Barry experienced a series of crushing blows on the work front. Financial distress plagued Karen and Barry's marriage. So to help make ends meet, Karen took a teaching job.

Amazingly though, during this difficult time Barry never questioned God. He always saw a brighter day on the horizon.

After moving from California to Wisconsin to Oregon, Barry began to feel that life was looking up. When he landed a job with a Christian firm, he had found his niche: coaching and consulting professionals in the mortgage industry. Barry felt that the prospect of a secure future for him, his wife, and their three boys was closer than ever before.

That's when the couple began noticing behavior problems with their eldest son. He struggled with mood swings more than most kids his age, which brought pain and hardship into Barry and Karen's life. Their hearts were torn with concern and sadness for their little guy. Things were totally out of their control.

Where is God in all this? Will He show up and save the day? When will it get better? These are some of the questions Barry and Karen asked—and keep asking.

Discussion Questions

a. How would you respond to these trials if you were Barry? How would you respond if you knew the situation wouldn't get resolved in this life?

b. What might your prayers sound like?

c. How do you account for the existence of pain and suffering in the lives of believers? Why do you think God allows it?

d. What would it look like for a man to be content in such situations? How might his "need to control" affect his contentment?

e. Share an experience you've had that caused you to wonder whether God was in charge.

f. Do you think every man has to have a Job-like experience to change his perspective about God? Why or why not?

g. How has this session helped you gain a new appreciation for God in the midst of life's uncontrollable circumstances?

Standing Strong

What worst-case scenario do you think would make it impossible for you to find contentment?

Now add the God factor to this scenario. How might knowing the end of Job's story help you be content even in the worst possible situation?

come clean with weakness

Living Content with Who You Really Are

Key Verse

He said to me, "My grace is sufficient for you, for my power is made perfect in weakness." Therefore I will boast all the more gladly about my weaknesses, so that Christ's power may rest on me. (2 Corinthians 12:9)

Goals for Growth

- Be willing to ruthlessly expose my weaknesses before the Lord.
- Receive the full impact of Jesus's grace in my life.
- Let my weaknesses drive me to God.

Head Start

Men gauge success by how well they are using their strengths. In fact, it's not uncommon to hear men boasting about them. I (Todd) have never heard a man say, "So, tell me about your weaknesses. How have they helped you succeed?" Generally, we cover up our limitations, hoping nobody will notice the chinks in our high-gloss armor.

In his book *Posers, Fakers, and Wannabes: Unmasking the Real You,* Brennan Manning points out that we naturally want to cover up and mask our real selves. It seems we put on a pretty convincing show. But underlying a man's posing is a deep sense of disappointment with the way God has made him. *Why did God make me so insecure about the way I look (or think or act or work)?* he wonders. *If I were just different, maybe more like Greg or Bob or Joe...*

One of the most disturbing facts about men today is their profound self-hatred. Men are far less tolerant of their own weaknesses than they are of other people's weaknesses. No wonder so many men prefer to keep themselves sedated.

But the truth is, God made you the way He did, weaknesses and all, so that you'd cling to the power of Christ for your daily survival. Weak men are dependent men. We would never learn to be content in Christ if we didn't have weaknesses. Our weaknesses help us find contentment outside ourselves.

Paul called his weakness "a thorn in [the] flesh" (2 Corinthians 12:7). What is your thorn? When does it plague you the most? And the critical question: Do you cover up your weakness at all costs? Your response to this last question will determine whether you are content with who you are.

Just as rose bushes come with thorns, so God's design for your life is incomplete without your thorns. One of my (Todd's) thorns is a weakness many men struggle with: the need to be in control. This weakness has plagued my marriage for seventeen years. It's rooted in a fear of what emotions might bubble up if I would just "be" rather than be in command.

How I've prayed to shuck this prickly menace! It causes me so much pain and discontentment. When I power up and take control of situations in my own strength, I lose every time. I hurt my wife and crush her spirit.

But I've found that when I am willing to reveal my weaknesses and admit my fears, Christ sends a wave of grace that covers me with His confidence and strength. Then I become more gracious toward others. Having seen such wonderful results, I'm becoming more open about my thorns these days.

So how can Christ's power be displayed mightily in you? It's all tied up with your ability to be content not only with your strengths but with your weaknesses as well. God has given them to you for a purpose. Let them do their work in your life.

Connect with the Word

Read 2 Corinthians 12:7-10.

1. Why is "thorn in [the] flesh" a good metaphor to describe the weaknesses that plague a man (verse 7)?

2. What do you consider to be your biggest thorn in the flesh? When, if ever, have you been thankful for this particular weakness?

3. The text says Paul prayed three times for the removal of his thorn (verse 8). Some Bible commentators think this was a way of saying, in Paul's culture, "I prayed constantly." What do you think is the significance of Paul's actions?

4. When have you most clearly seen God's power made perfect in your weakness? What was your feeling toward God at that time?

5. Find a good definition of *grace* in a Bible dictionary or from an online source (such as *crosswalk.com* or *www.blueletterbible.org*). How does this definition help you understand that contentment is found only in Christ?

6. Can you extend grace to others if you've never allowed yourself to receive it? Explain. (Include a personal example,
   if possible.)

7. In your own words, explain the truth of Paul's concluding
   paradox, "When I am weak, then I am strong" (verse 10). How
   can you apply this truth to help you face a looming difficulty in
   your life?

Connect with the Group

Group Opener
Read the group opener aloud and discuss the questions that follow.

Dear Tech Support:
Last year I upgraded from Boyfriend 5.0 to Husband 1.0 and noticed
a distinct slowdown in overall performance, particularly in the flower

and jewelry applications, which operated flawlessly under Boyfriend 5.0.

In addition, Husband 1.0 uninstalled many other valuable programs, such as Romance 9.5 and Personal Attention 6.5. It then installed undesirable programs such as NFL 5.0, NHL 4.3, MLB 3.0, and NBA 3.6.

Conversation 8.0 no longer runs, and Housecleaning 2.6 simply crashed the system. I've tried running Nag-Nag 5.3 to fix these problems, to no avail. What can I do?

Signed,

Desperate

Dear Desperate:

First, keep in mind that Boyfriend 5.0 is an entertainment package, while Husband 1.0 is an operating system. Try entering the command: c:/ithoughtyoulovedme in order to download Tears 6.2, which should automatically install Guilt 3.0. If that application works as designed, Husband 1.0 should then automatically run the applications Jewelry 2.0 and Flowers 3.5.

Remember, though, that overuse of the above application can cause Husband 1.0 to default to Grumpy Silence 2.5, Happy Hour 7.0, or Beer 6.1. (Beer 6.1 is a very bad program that will create Snoring Loudly 10.8.)

No matter what, do not install Mother-in-Law 1.0 or reinstall another Boyfriend program. These are not supported applications and will crash Husband 1.0.

In summary, Husband 1.0 is a great program, but it does have limited memory and cannot learn new applications quickly. You might consider buying additional software to improve memory and performance. I personally recommend Hot Food 3.0 and Lingerie 7.7.

Good luck,

Tech Support[1]

What is your reaction to this humorous e-mail? Tell the other guys about one "application weakness" related to your marriage or a current dating relationship.

Discussion Questions

a. How does marriage bring out our weaknesses, perhaps thorns we never thought we had?

---

1. This e-mail can be found on numerous Internet sites. Original source is unknown.

b. Do you think every man has a thorn in the flesh? Why or why not? What do you think yours might be? Explain.

c. What do you think boasting about your weaknesses looks like?

d. Why do you think we feel so compelled to pose and fake to hide our weaknesses?

e. Have you ever experienced a time when God gave you a sense of contentment after you fully accepted an area of weakness? Explain.

f. Do you pose and fake with the Lord when you pray, or do you openly express your weaknesses to Him? Explain. (*Suggestion:* Open your heart and talk with the Lord about it.)

g. Rate your group on a "thorn scale" from 1 to 5 "sharp" points (1 = dull and 5 = razor sharp). Ask yourselves, To what extent is our group willing to be honest with one another about our weaknesses?

What can you do as a group to promote more honesty with one another in this area?

Standing Strong

Complete the sentence below, then ask the man next to you to pray that you might accept your thorn from the Lord. Do the same for him. Pray together that you will allow this weakness to make you more content in Christ's power alone.

My big thorn in the flesh is _____.

mission possible

Finding a Mission That Brings Contentment

Key Verse

I became a servant of this gospel by the gift of God's grace given me through the working of his power. (Ephesians 3:7)

Goals for Growth

- Gain a new identity for my life.
- Focus on a mission for my life that counts.
- Live with more purpose each day.

Head Start

How would you describe your mission in life? How about your core identity—the way you view yourself? These two questions always go together because a man will never find his mission in life until he knows his core identity. How you see yourself will determine the course of your whole life. Mission flows from identity.

When we become confused about our mission in life, discontentment reigns. There's nothing more frustrating than trying to live out a mission that God never intended for us. That's because our true mission comes from God. Finding it is the most compelling factor in our lives, and we'll never be content until we do find it.

Let's go to the cineplex with this idea. Do you agree that the greatest "guy movies" are about men who have found their identity and mission in life? They carry out their mission with such passion and fortitude that we wish we could jump through the screen and enter the action ourselves.

There is nothing more compelling than seeing a man who is focused on his mission. Whether we're watching Ben-Hur or William Wallace, we see a mission flowing from an identity. Ben-Hur refused to compromise his Jewish beliefs and sell out to the Roman Empire. Wallace was a Scot who refused to allow the British to own his country. He was unwilling to compromise with freedom—and it cost him his life.

The Passion of the Christ by Mel Gibson (the actor who played William Wallace in *Braveheart*) is probably the most graphic depiction of the life of Christ ever produced on film, so graphic that many viewers were appalled. The American public can apparently handle the depiction of a man like William Wallace who was so focused on his mission that it led to his death, but people don't know what to do with Christ whose mission was so God-focused that He was willing to endure scourging and crucifixion to save the world.

If you see yourself merely as a member of the work force, that's who you will be: a worker. If you see yourself as the sole provider for your family, that will be your mission in life: to provide. If you see yourself as a defeated Christian man who will never enjoy spiritual maturity, chances are you won't grow in Christ. But if you know clearly who you are—a child of God, profoundly loved, secure for all eternity—you will discover your mission, and your life will become an adventure worthy of five-star reviews. Paul was that kind of man. Like Ben-Hur, Wallace, and our Lord Jesus, he was deeply aware of who he was and became consumed with his God-given mission.

How is it with you? Have you entered the action scene yet?

Connect with the Word

Read Ephesians 3:1-9.

1. List some of the ways Paul identified his mission in life and his core identity. (*Suggestion:* Look at this passage in the New American Standard Bible to answer this question).

Paul's Mission	*Paul's Identity*

2. How do you think Paul's sense of identity affected his purpose and direction in life? What clues do you find in this Scripture passage? (Include key words and phrases from the passage in your response.)

3. What seemed most important to Paul: his comfort or his mission? How can you tell? (Include key words and phrases from the passage in your response.)

4. Why is it easy for men today to become more focused on comfort than on the mission adventure God is calling us to?

5. What fear might we experience when faced with our true identity—and the mission that comes with it?

Read 2 Corinthians 4:8-12,16-18.

6. How was Paul able to reconcile his identity in Christ with the way he was treated?

7. What effect do you think this ability had on Paul's level of contentment?

8. What would have to change in your life for you to become more like Paul in this regard? (Be as specific as possible.)

Connect with the Group

Group Opener
Read the group opener aloud and discuss the questions that follow.

Jim Elliot felt called to reach the Auca Indians of South America with the good news of Christ. His motto was, "He is no fool who gives up what he cannot keep to gain what he cannot lose." Though he was martyred before he was able to accomplish his mission, his wife, Elisabeth, took up the cause and did complete it. Eventually, the men who killed Jim came to Christ and grew strong in the faith, leading their entire village into the kingdom.

Here is an entry from Jim's journal on July 11, 1952, before he died at the hands of men he loved unconditionally with the love of Christ:

> How well I see now that He is wanting to do something in me!
> So many missionaries, intent on doing something, forget that
> His main work is to make something of them, not just to do a
> work by their stiff and bungling fingers. Teach me, Lord Jesus,
> to live simply and love purely, like a child, and to know that
> You are unchanged in Your attitudes and actions toward me.
> Give me not to be hungering for the strange, rare, and peculiar
> when the common, ordinary, and regular—rightly taken—will
> suffice to feed and satisfy the soul. Bring struggle when I need
> it; take away ease at Your pleasure.[2]

Discussion Questions

a. What is your gut reaction to the story of Jim Elliot?

---

2. Elizabeth Elliot, *Shadow of the Almighty: The Life and Testament of Jim Elliot* (New York: HarperCollins, 1979), 179.

b. Do you believe it's possible for you to have the same level of mission passion that Jim Elliot had? Why or why not?

c. From the Bible passages you've studied in this session, what new insights have you gained about your core identity? Has your identity changed? Has your mission become clearer? In what ways?

d. What steps do you plan to take to better align your core identity with your life mission?

e. How will this alignment likely bring about greater contentment in your life?

Standing Strong

Write out some of the key components of your personal mission statement. Following are some phrases to get you started. (*Note:* If you are still searching for your mission, then use this exercise as a call to prayer. Ask God to guide you and give you a clear sense of your true identity and calling in His kingdom.)

I am a man resolved to. . .

I see myself serving the Lord by. . .

I want to be the spiritual leader of my family by. . .

I desire to reach others for Christ by. . .

watch out for out of bounds!

Getting Rid of That Fleshy Discontent

Key Verse

So I say, live by the Spirit, and you will not gratify the desires of the sinful nature. (Galatians 5:16)

Goals for Growth

- Recognize signs of fleshly living.
- Learn to yield to the leading of the Spirit.
- Embrace the Spirit's influence in my life.

Head Start

Skiing in Jackson Hole, Wyoming, is risky business. It's not for the weak at heart. The abundant, marked terrain is dangerous and steep, even though these runs have been tested by the ski patrol and cleared of all life-threatening hazards. There are, however, dozens of off-limit signs and yellow tape blocking paths that lead to avalanche danger, loose rocks, and cliffs.

Of course, people can choose to ignore the signs and duck under the tape. I (Todd) once watched a couple of hot doggers head off into the trees, with danger clearly in sight. I even debated whether to try it myself—maybe it would be the run of a lifetime…or the stupidest thing I'd ever done. Actually, I wanted desperately to go for it. But I'm no longer eighteen, and I'm a lot wiser than I once was, so I chose not to follow those guys. Great survival stories come from out-of-bounds living, but not all of them end well.

The Christian life is a lot like the terrain at Jackson Hole. There are plenty of marked runs and rugged terrain to keep the most adventuresome man entertained and motivated. Yes, there's plenty of room to run in the Christian life. But there are hazardous areas to avoid if we don't want to get hurt. Our flesh calls out to us to swerve toward those enticing out-of-bounds runs. It wants nothing more than to hurtle us over a cliff and end our witness.

Get it straight now. The most discontent man around is the one who's still wrestling with his flesh. If you're standing on the precipice of an out-of-bounds run—or if you are already heading down one—you're discontent to the max. Sin has gotten the best of you, and you are in for more than a thrilling ride. You're in for death!

In Galatians 5, Paul says that we either go the way of the flesh or we go the way of the Spirit. He doesn't mean they are equal forces in a man's life, but he does say it's a choice each of us has to make: spiritual death or spiritual life.

So stay in bounds. Go the way of the Spirit. There is plenty of adventure on that path. One of the common misunderstandings about the Christian life is that it is boring and Christians just don't know how to have fun. Who are we kidding? The Spirit of God offers a different way down the mountain. It's still plenty steep—but it leads to unending joy.

Connect with the Word

Read Galatians 5:16-26.

1. How well does your flesh get along with the Holy Spirit who lives inside of you? Explain.

2. Which is more powerful: the flesh or the Spirit? How do you know? (See also 1 John 4:4.)

3. Which takes more power: to get even or to be at peace with someone who hates your guts? To explode with anger or to

return kindness to a boss who has just undermined your position with the company? Explain your answers.

4. What are the practical differences between walking in the flesh and walking in the Spirit?

5. What helps you avoid the pitfalls of walking according to the flesh? What role does your men's group play?

6. Paul said that the flesh wages a war with our souls and tries to ambush our witness for Christ (verse 17). Since we can't make the flesh go away, the best we can do is counter its power with a force that is even greater: the Holy Spirit. When have you found

the power of the Holy Spirit to be greater than the power of your temptation? (*Suggestion:* Be ready to share this story with the guys in your group.)

Connect with the Group

Group Opener
Read the group opener aloud and discuss the questions that follow.

Many men feel discontent in life because they live defeated and ashamed. They keep losing the battle with temptation and sin. On the other hand, when we master sin, we find contentment.

In *The Twin Towers,* the second book of J. R. R. Tolkien's The Lord of the Rings series, Gollum, a worn-down, grotesque-looking creature, is in a raging battle with his desires. Two identities within him struggle for control. The Gollum part of him desperately desires the dark influence of the ring of power and tries to seize the ring from Frodo. The Sméagol part of him, the hobbitlike creature Gollum used to be, wants to win this battle and help Frodo destroy the ring and its destructive power.

Tolkien uses this conflicted character to reveal the sin influence that can take down even the most innocent person. In his final book, *The Return of the King,* Tolkien leaves us wondering how Gollum will fare against the dark influence of the ring and which voice inside him will ultimately win.

Every man battles his flesh on a daily basis. As with Gollum, a voice within taunts him to cave in and live out of the flesh. This voice leads him far from where he truly desires to be: content in Spirit living. He presses on, but the voice keeps calling to him in the deep recesses of his soul: "Come on, you deserve this!" "It's not your fault." "You can't help yourself." "It will all work out." But sin never works out.

Only the man completely influenced by the Holy Spirit stands a chance against the sinful ways of the flesh.

Discussion Questions

a. Do you think Christian theology can be communicated effectively in books, films, and other analogical approaches? Why or why not? If you've read the series or seen the films, how well do you think The Lord of the Rings does in this area?

b. What does it take for a man to turn control of his life over to the Spirit, especially when he's experiencing intense temptation? What has worked best for you at these times? What advice would you give to the other men about this?

c. What sin issues are most tempting for you? What can the other men in your group do to help you avoid going out of bounds— going the way of the flesh?

d. How does walking in the Spirit, as described in Galatians 5:16-26, counter the pull of the flesh and bring a deep sense of contentment?

e. "He's lost another battle with the flesh." Is there any greater feeling of discontentment? any worse heartache? any deeper guilt and frustration? When a man falls to temptation, he feels like a loser. Based on the passage you just studied, how would you counsel a friend who feels this way?

f. Talk about your response to the final question in Connect with the Word. When have you experienced the Holy Spirit's power to carry you through the toughest temptations?

Standing Strong

Write a prayer to the Holy Spirit. Honestly reveal where you are with out-of-bounds behaviors. Invite the Spirit to show you a new way to go. Then spend some time in silence…listening.

small-group resources

leader tips

What if men aren't doing the Connect with the Word section before our small-group session?

Don't be discouraged. You set the pace. If you are doing the study and regularly referring to it in conversations with your men throughout the week, they will pick up on its importance. Here are some suggestions to motivate the men in your group to do their home Bible study:

- Send out a midweek e-mail in which you share your answer to one of the study questions. This shows them that you are personally committed to and involved in the study.
- Ask the guys to hit Respond to All on their e-mail program and share one insight from that week's Bible study with the entire group. Encourage them to send it out before the next small-group session.
- Every time you meet, ask each man in the group to share one insight from his home study.

What if men are not showing up for small group?

This might mean they are losing a sin battle and don't want to admit it to the group. Or they might be consumed with other priorities. Or maybe they don't think they're getting anything out of the group. Here are some suggestions for getting the guys back each week:

- Affirm them when they show up, and tell them how much it means to you that they make small group a priority.

- From time to time, ask them to share one reason small group is important to them.
- Regularly call or send out an e-mail the day before you meet to remind them you're looking forward to seeing them.
- Check in with any guy who has missed more than one session and find out what's going on in his life.
- Get some feedback from the men. You may need to adjust your style. Listen and learn.

What if group discussion is not happening?

You are a discussion facilitator. You have to keep guys involved in the discussion or you'll lose them. You can engage a man who isn't sharing by saying, "Chuck, you've been quiet. What do you think about this question or discussion?" You should also be prepared to share your own personal stories that are related to the discussion questions. You'll set the example by the kind of sharing you do.

What if one man is dominating the group time?

You have to deal with it. If you don't, men will stop showing up. No one wants to hear from just one guy all the time. It will quickly kill morale. Meet with the guy in person and privately. Firmly but gently suggest that he allow others more time to talk. Be positive and encouraging, but truthful. You might say, "Bob, I notice how enthusiastic you are about the group and how you're always prepared to share your thoughts with the group. But there are some pretty quiet guys in the group too. Have you noticed? Would you be willing to help me get them involved in speaking up?"

How do I get the guys in my group more involved?
Give them something to do. Ask one guy to bring a snack. Invite another to lead the prayer time (ask in advance). Have a guy sub for you one week as the leader. (Meet with him beforehand to walk through the group program and the time allotments for each segment.) Encourage another guy to lead a subgroup.

What if guys are not being vulnerable during the Standing Strong or prayer times?
You model openness. You set the pace. Honesty breeds honesty. Vulnerability breeds vulnerability. Are you being vulnerable and honest about your own problems and struggles? (This doesn't mean that you have to spill your guts each week or reveal every secret of your life.) Remember, men want an honest, on-their-level leader who strives to walk with God. (Also, as the leader, you need an accountability partner, perhaps another group leader.)

What will we do at the first session?
We encourage you to open by discussing the **Small-Group Covenant** we've included in this resource section. Ask the men to commit to the study, and then discuss how long it will take your group to complete each session. (We suggest 75-90 minute sessions.) Men find it harder to come up with excuses for missing a group session if they have made a covenant to the other men right at the start.

Begin to identify ways certain men can play a more active role in small group. Give away responsibility. You won't feel as burdened, and your men will grow from the experience. Keep in mind that this process can take a few weeks. Challenge men to fulfill one of the group roles identified later in this resource section. If no one steps forward to fill a role, say to one of the men, "George, I've noticed that you are comfortable praying in a group. Would you lead us each week during that time?"

How can we keep the group connected after we finish a study?
Begin talking about starting another Bible study before you finish this eight-week study. (There are several other studies to choose from in the Every Man Bible study series.) Consider having a social time at the conclusion of the study, and encourage the men to invite a friend. This will help create momentum and encourage growth as you launch into another study with your group. There are probably many men in your church or neighborhood who aren't in small groups but would like to be. Be the kind of group that includes others.

As your group grows, consider choosing an apprentice leader who can take half the group into another room for the **Connect with the Group** time. That subgroup can stay together for prayer, or you can reconvene as a large group during that time. You could also meet for discussion as a large group and then break into subgroups for **Standing Strong** and **prayer.**

If your group doubles in size, it might be a perfect opportunity to release your apprentice leader with half the group to start another group. Allow men to pray about this and make a decision as a group. Typically, the relational complexities that come into play when a small group births a new group work themselves out. Allow guys to choose which group they'd like to be a part of. If guys are slow in choosing one group or another, ask them individually to select one of the groups. Take the lead in making this happen.

Look for opportunities for your group to serve in the church or community. Consider a local outreach project or a short-term missions trip. There are literally hundreds of practical ways you can serve the Lord in outreach. Check with your church leaders to learn the needs in your congregation or community. Create some interest by sending out scouts who will return with a report for the group. Serving keeps men from becoming self-focused and ingrown. When you serve as a group, you will grow as a group.

using this study in a large-group format

Many church leaders are looking for biblically based curriculum that can be used in a large-group setting, such as a Sunday-school class, or for small groups within an existing larger men's group. Each of the Every Man Bible studies can be adapted for this purpose. In addition, this curriculum can become a catalyst for churches wishing to launch men's small groups or to build a men's ministry.

Getting Started

Begin by getting the word out to men in your church, inviting them to join you for a men's study based on one of the topics in the Every Man Bible study series. You can place a notice in your church bulletin, have the pastor announce it from the pulpit, or pursue some other means of attracting interest.

Orientation Week

Arrange your room with round tables and chairs. Put approximately six chairs at each table.

Start your session in prayer and introduce your topic with a short but motivational message from any of the scriptures used in the Bible study. Hand out the curriculum and challenge the men to do their homework before each session. During this first session give the men some discussion questions based upon an overview of the material and have them talk things through within their small group around the table.

Just before you wrap things up, have each group select a table host or leader. You can do this by having everyone point at once to the person at their table they feel would best facilitate discussion for future meetings.

Ask those newly elected table leaders to stay after for a few minutes, and offer them an opportunity to be further trained as small-group leaders as they lead discussions throughout the course of the study.

Subsequent Weeks

Begin in prayer. Then give a short message (15-25 minutes) based upon the scripture used for that lesson. Pull out the most motivating topics or points, and strive to make the discussion relevant to the everyday life and world of a typical man. Then leave time for each table to work through the discussion questions listed in the curriculum. Be sure the discussion facilitators at each table close in prayer.

At the end of the eight sessions, you might want to challenge each "table group" to become a small group, inviting them to meet regularly with their new small-group leader and continue building the relationships they've begun.

prayer request record

Date:
Name:
Prayer Request:
Praise:

Date:
Name:
Prayer Request:
Praise:

Date:
Name:
Prayer Request:
Praise:

Date:
Name:
Prayer Request:
Praise:

Date:
Name:
Prayer Request:
Praise:

defining group roles

Group Leader: Leads the lesson and facilitates group discussion.

Apprentice Leader: Assists the leader as needed, which may include leading the lesson.

Refreshment Coordinator: Maintains a list of who will provide refreshments. Calls group members on the list to remind them to bring what they signed up for.

Prayer Warrior: Serves as the contact person for prayer between sessions. Establishes a list of those willing to pray for needs that arise. Maintains the prayer-chain list and activates the chain as needed by calling the first person on the list.

Social Chairman: Plans any desired social events during group sessions or at another scheduled time. Gathers members for planning committees as needed.

small-group roster

Name:
Address:
Phone: E-mail:

Name:
Address:
Phone: E-mail:

Name:
Address:
Phone: E-mail:

Name:
Address:
Phone: E-mail:

Name:
Address:
Phone: E-mail:

Name:
Address:
Phone: E-mail:

spiritual checkup

Your answers to the statements below will help you determine which areas you need to work on in order to grow spiritually. Mark the appropriate letter to the left of each statement. Then make a plan to take one step toward further growth in each area. Don't forget to pray for the Lord's wisdom before you begin. Be honest. Don't be overly critical or rationalize your weaknesses.

Y = Yes
S = Somewhat or Sometimes
N = No

My Spiritual Connection with Other Believers

____ I am developing relationships with Christian friends.
____ I have joined a small group.
____ I am dealing with conflict in a biblical manner.
____ I have become more loving and forgiving than I was a year ago.
____ I am a loving and devoted husband and father.

My Spiritual Growth

____ I have committed to daily Bible reading and prayer.
____ I am journaling on a regular basis, recording my spiritual growth.

____ I am growing spiritually by studying the Bible with others.

____ I am honoring God in my finances and personal giving.

____ I am filled with joy and gratitude for my life, even during trials.

____ I respond to challenges with peace and faith instead of anxiety and anger.

____ I avoid addictive behaviors (excessive drinking, overeating, watching too much TV, etc.).

Serving Christ and Others

____ I am in the process of discovering my spiritual gifts and talents.

____ I am involved in ministry in my church.

____ I have taken on a role or responsibility in my small group.

____ I am committed to helping someone else grow in his spiritual walk.

Sharing Christ with Others

____ I care about and am praying for those around me who are unbelievers.

____ I share my experience of coming to know Christ with others.

____ I invite others to join me in this group or for weekend worship services.

____ I am praying for others to come to Christ and am seeing this happen.

____ I do what I can to show kindness to people who don't know Christ.

Surrendering My Life for Growth

___ I attend church services weekly.

___ I pray for others to know Christ, and I seek to fulfill the Great Commission.

___ I regularly worship God through prayer, praise, and music, both at church and at home.

___ I care for my body through exercise, nutrition, and rest.

___ I am concerned about using my energy to serve God's purposes instead of my own.

My Identity in the Lord

___ I see myself as a beloved son of God, one whom God loves regardless of my sin.

___ I can come to God in all of my humanity and know that He accepts me completely. When I fail, I willingly run to God for forgiveness.

___ I experience Jesus as an encouraging Friend and Lord each moment of the day.

___ I have an abiding sense that God is on my side. I am aware of His gracious presence with me throughout the day.

___ During moments of beauty, grace, and human connection, I lift up praise and thanks to God.

___ I believe that using my talents to their fullest pleases the Lord.

___ I experience God's love for me in powerful ways.

small-group covenant

As a committed group member, I agree to the following:*

- **Regular Attendance.** I will attend group sessions on time and let everyone know in advance if I can't make it.
- **Group Safety.** I will help create a safe, encouraging environment where men can share their thoughts and feelings without fear of embarrassment or rejection. I will not judge other guys or attempt to fix their problems.
- **Confidentiality.** I will always keep to myself everything that is shared in the group.
- **Acceptance.** I will respect different opinions or beliefs and let Scripture be the teacher.
- **Accountability.** I will make myself accountable to the other group members for the personal goals I share.
- **Friendliness.** I will look for those around me who might join the group and explore their faith with other men.
- **Ownership.** I will prayerfully consider taking on a specific role within the group as the opportunity arises.
- **Spiritual Growth.** I will commit to establishing a daily quiet time with God, which includes doing the homework for this study. I will share with the group the progress I make and the struggles I experience as I seek to grow spiritually.

Signed: _____ Date: _____

* Permission is given to photocopy and distribute this form to each man in your group. Review this covenant quarterly or as needed.

start a bible study
and connect with others
who want to be God's man.

Every Man Bible Studies are designed to help you discover, own, and build
on convictions grounded in God's word. Available now in bookstores.

WATERBROOK
PRESS

about the authors

STEPHEN ARTERBURN is coauthor of the best-selling Every Man series. He is also founder and chairman of New Life Clinics, host of the daily *New Life Live!* national radio program, and creator of the Women of Faith conferences. A nationally known speaker and licensed minister, Stephen has authored more than forty books. He lives with his family in Laguna Beach, California.

KENNY LUCK is president and founder of Every Man Ministries, coauthor of *Every Man, God's Man* and its companion workbook, and coauthor of the Every Man Bible studies. He is the area leader for men's ministry and teaches a men's interactive Bible study at Saddleback Church in Lake Forest, California. He and his wife, Chrissy, have three children and reside in Trabuco Canyon, California.

TODD WENDORFF is a graduate of University of California, Berkeley, and holds a ThM from Talbot School of Theology. He serves as a teaching pastor at King's Harbor Church in Redondo Beach and is an adjunct professor at Biola University. He is an author of the Doing Life Together Bible study series. Todd and his wife, Denise, live with their three children in Rolling Hills Estates, California.